"The Guy Who Lost His Beach House"

One-Minute Bible Parables for Kids

"The Guy Who Lost His Beach House"

One-Minute Bible Parables for Kids

Written by Marnie Wooding

Illustrated by Chris Kielesinski

HOLMAN
BIBLE PUBLISHERS

Nashville, Tennessee

"The Guy Who Lost His Beach House"
One-Minute Bible Parables for Kids

© Copyright 2000 Lightwave Publishing Inc.
All Rights Reserved

ISBN 0-8054-9398-0
Dewey Decimal Classification: 226.8
Subject Heading: Juvenile literature

For Lightwave
Concept Design and Direction: *Rick Osborne*
Managing Editor: *Elaine Osborne*
Text Director: *K. Christie Bowler*
Art Director: *Terry Van Roon*
Desktop: *Andrew Jaster*

The Holman Christian Standard Bible
© Copyright 1999, 2000 Holman Bible Publishers

Library of Congress Cataloging-in-Publication Data
Wooding, Marnie
    The guy who lost his beach house / written by Marnie Wooding ; illustrated by Chris Kielesinski.
    p. cm.
    ISBN 0-8054-9398-0 (alk. paper)
    1. Parables—Juvenile literature [1. Parables. 2. Bible stories—N.T.] I. Kielesinski, Chris, ill. II. Title.

BT376 .W66 2000
226.8'09505—dc21
                    00-037828

Bibliography of Sources

After School Weird Stuff Brain Quest. New York: Workman Publishing Company, 1996.
"Encarta 98," CD-ROM Microsoft Corporation.
Matthews, Peter and Norris McWhirter. *The Guinness Book of Records 1993*. Middlesex, England: Guinness Publishing, 1993.
Matthews, Victor H. *Manners and Customs in the Bible*. Rev. ed. Peabody, Massachusetts: Hendrickson Publishers Inc, 1996.
Millard, Alan. *Nelson's Illustrated Wonders and Discoveries of the Bible*. Nashville: Thomas Nelson Publishers, 1997.
Penwell, Dan. *Bible Brain Quest 1,000 Questions & Answers About the Old & New Testaments*. New York: Workman Publishing Company, 1997.
Rosenbloom, Joseph. *The Little Giant Book of Riddles*. New York: Sterling Publishing Co. Inc., 1996.
Seyffert, Oskar. *Dictionary of Classical Antiquities*. Cleveland: Meridian Books, 1969.
Wallechinsky, David and Amy Wallace. *The Book of Lists*. Boston: Little, Brown and Company, 1995.
Werner, Keller. *The Bible As History*. 2nd Rev. ed. New York: Bantam Books, 1988.
The Youth Bible—New Century Version. Dallas: Word Publishing, 1991.

Printed in Korea
1 2 3 4 5 04 03 02 01 00
SW

Contents

Introduction

Oh, hi! Great to see you! I'm your narrator, and I've been waiting for you to open this book! The introduction is the beginning of the book, so I thought it would be the perfect time to get to know one another. What's a narrator? Well, I'm the person who explains the stories (parables in this case) in a funny and approachable way. (The publisher told me to say that.) What I'm really here for is for us to have a great time as I tell you about the parables or stories that Jesus told a long, long time ago. I'm supposed to tell you each story in one minute, so I sure hope you're a *superfast* reader! Just kidding. Don't worry, I'll always go at your pace.

Why did Jesus tell us stories? Simple! Jesus understood that there is a lot of interesting stuff to learn about God. So, to help us understand His Father in heaven better, He told not just stories, but GREAT stories. As a matter of fact, these stories are full of hidden treasure. What kind of treasure, you ask? Well, to discover THAT you'll have to journey through the parables with me.

In the course of our journey you will also learn some important sayings from the Bible, and we'll ask a few puzzling questions. I'm also going to tell you a few jokes along the way. (Just a note for the future—if you, the reader, laugh at the narrator's jokes, it always makes the narrator feel good about herself. Cheering and clapping are, of course, optional.) Now that we've gotten the introductions over with, why don't we start exploring the parables?

The Guy Who Lost His Beach House

"Therefore, everyone who hears these words of Mine and acts on them will be like a sensible man who built his house on the rock" (Matthew 7:24).

Jesus told a story about two men who decided to build homes for themselves. He didn't give us a lot of details on the men, but I imagine, since they were Israelites, they likely had names like Bilhan or Aran. Let's try those names on for size.

Aran, *"a sensible man,"* probably looked around for a good plot of land to build his house on. I figure he found it right on top of a great, big, solid piece of rock! I don't think it was easy, but Aran did it right. He must have dug and chiseled, bricked and hammered until he had an "A" Number 1 perfect house built from stone walls to thatched roof. You could say it was rock solid!

Now, Bilhan, *"the foolish man,"* had different ideas. It seems he just did his own thing and didn't waste any time looking around for a good piece of ground. I think he's the type of guy that would have grabbed the first piece of terra firma—I mean land—he stumbled upon to put his fancy dream beach house on. Jesus tells us Bilhan built on sand, so maybe he built his beach house by a river like the great Jordan River, and maybe it had a deck right by the water, next to his private pier. Sounds great, doesn't it? Welllll, the only problem, which was plain to anybody who had eyes to see, was that the ground where Bilhan built his house was too . . . too sandy. A sad case of terra firma that wasn't very firma! But oooh no, this didn't seem to bother old Bilhan. He built his house anyway.

Everything seemed to work out well for the guys. That is, until the storm came. *"The rain fell, the rivers rose"* (Matthew 7:25). I think it rained so hard even the fish didn't like it. The rivers just got bigger and wilder.

Well, the rain sure beat down on Aran's house. The shutters rattled and

DIDYAKNOW?

Most houses were very simple in Jesus' time. One large room was used for the kitchen, daily activities, and sleeping. Some homes may also have had small workrooms and a tiny room to bathe in.

the chimney whistled—*"the winds blew and pounded that house"* (Matthew 7:25). But when the storm was over, his house stood just as straight and solid as the rock it was built upon.

What about Bilhan? Sad to report, the flood washed the sand right out from beneath his fancy beach house and the entire thing hit the dirt, or should I say sand, plaster flooring to wood beams. *"And its collapse was great!"* (Matthew 7:27). Last seen, it was probably floating down the river like a raft with Bilhan sitting on top. Okay, okay, the Bible doesn't exactly say that it was floating down the river. But it could

JOKE

What did one pile of sand ask the other pile of sand? *"What're you dune?"*

have been if we use our imaginations.

Now, there's something to be learned from Aran and Bilhan, and not just about building houses. Jesus wanted us to learn about listening to God's Word and doing things right. You could say wise Aran built his life on the solid rock that was Jesus' teaching and put what he learned into practice. I mean he was honest, kind, did his homework, listened to his parents, respected his elders—he was just an all-around great guy! Not-too-smart Bilhan was like a man who'd heard God's teaching, but he just plain up and did things his own way. And his way, as we found out, was a long raft ride to nowhere! He was down the creek without a paddle. *"But everyone who hears these words of Mine and doesn't act on them will be like a fool-*

ish man who built his house on sand" (Matthew 7:26). He was the type of guy who rolled his eyes at his parents, neglected his chores, walked around with a major ego head, and was completely unreliable. When you try to take shortcuts or do things your own way, like Bilhan, nothing is going to work out right, and you won't be able to do the things God wants you to do. Why? Because you'll be too busy fixing big mistakes, just like Bilhan.

How can you be an Aran instead of a Bilhan? Well, you can start by building your "home" or life right: love Jesus and trust Him, and do things His way—you know, obey your parents, be kind to your neighbors, and be honest in all things. In every situation stop and think, "What would Jesus want me to do?" Remember that God loves you! When you do things His way, they will work out. So, read the Bible, learn what Jesus says is right, and do it. That's what I call really rock'n on!

QUESTION CORNER

* Why should you learn Jesus' teachings?
* Is God's way of living always right? Why or why not?
* Tell me a story about when you did things God's way. What happened? How did it work out and what did you learn from your experience?

JOKE

Where do rivers sleep? *In riverbeds!*

Too Seedy for Me!

"But the ones sown on good ground are those who hear the word, welcome it, and produce a crop" (Mark 4:20).

Jesus told a story about a sower of seeds. What's a sower? A farmer or worker who plants crop seeds in his field. (Back then, don't forget, they didn't even use a sowing machine. Get it?) Anyway, Jesus told a lot of farming parables because many of the people listening to him WERE farmers.

In this story a certain farmer was busy planting his crops for the season, perhaps barley or wheat. Every couple of minutes as he walked over his field, he would reach into his seed sack, gather a handful of seeds, and sprinkle them across the field.

"As he sowed, this occurred: Some seed fell along the path" (Mark 4:4). Instead of falling into the field's safe furrows of dirt, some seeds fell on the exposed dust of a pathway. Watch out!

Heads up! "And the birds came and ate it up" (Mark 4:4). Flap, peck, gulp . . . burp!

DIDYAKNOW?
The name "Jesus" means "The Lord saves."

Other seeds found a different fate! "Other seed fell on rocky ground where it didn't have much soil" (Mark 4:5). Sure, the seeds "sprang up right away, since it didn't have deep soil" (Mark 4:5), but hold on to your sunscreen! "When the sun came up, it was scorched, and since it didn't have a root, it withered" (Mark 4:6). Not very cool, if you get what I mean.

Our third group didn't fare any better, because they fell in with a bad crowd! "Other seed fell among thorns" (Mark 4:7). The young plants found themselves in a tight spot—they grew up, but the weedy thorns literally crowded them out!

This farmer's crop doesn't seem to be doing very well, does it? But, before you get all choked up about it—keep reading. Surprise! Other seeds did fall on good soil, just like they were supposed to. "Still others fell on good ground and produced a crop that increased thirty, sixty, and a hundred times" (Mark 4:8). Let's root for the home team!

So, you're thinking, that's nice for

the farmer, but what has that got to do with me? Funny you should ask, because Jesus' friends asked the same thing! The interesting thing about Jesus' stories is that people and things aren't always what they seem. Take our farmer friend. Jesus taught that the farmer was really like someone who taught God's Word. You know, like a preacher or perhaps a teacher. What were the seeds? Not seeds at all! They were the Word of God that was taught. And the different kinds of ground were like different kinds of people who heard the Word.

DIDYAKNOW?
A single winter rye plant can produce 387 miles worth of roots.

Take the example of the seeds that fell on the path. If we're not careful, we can expose ourselves to wrong things and become vulnerable. We hear God's teaching, but Satan, like the birds, takes what we learned away from us. How does he do that? Let's look at the other seed situations to find some ways we can save our learning.

"The ones sown on rocky ground: when they hear the word, immediately they receive it with joy. But they have no root in themselves; they are short-lived" (Mark 4:16–17). That's right, they just don't have what it takes to stick to it. They learn about God, but then quickly forget all they learned. You could say they can't soak it up because they have no roots.

What is our *"rocky ground"*? Trouble, worry, and being picked on can be three very uncomfortable pebbles in our lives. But we don't want to lose faith in God when we encounter troubles. Sometimes when you struggle with big problems at home or school, you forget that there is no situation in your life that God can't help you with. God is the situation specialist. He knows just what to do in any circumstance. God loves you! So trust Him in all things. Constant worry should go out with the birds.

Persecution sometimes takes the form of peer pressure. *"Don't follow the crowd when they do wrong"* (Exodus 23:2). We need to stay true to the things God wants us to do, even if it means not going to that blockbuster movie because we know it doesn't have right ideas or values. Instead, hang out with friends who like to do right things! You could say they're the right crowd. (For me that would be like sitting down with a good book.) When we do—we feel good about ourselves and our relationship with God.

What are the thorny weeds in our lives? The prickles of greed and desires. Ouch! They hurt! We get all wrapped up with daily activities and stuff. For example, we want to be the best hockey players on the team. Oops, we let our practice time slide into our time at home or with God. We get so busy saving for that new mountain bike, we forget to give to the needy. We simply let distractions clog our walk with God.

Suddenly, we don't have time to read the Bible or to learn the good

TRIVIA

How much did the good seed produce in this story? *A hundred times more than what was sown.*

things God wants us to know so we can have a happy life. Our need for God just sort of disappears. Jesus wanted us to know that we can't grow like that! We need to bury our roots deep in God's teaching and the life He has planned for us without any distractions or temptations. Do this and, hey, that good crop will be us!

QUESTION CORNER

* What sorts of things can you do each day to help you be part of the good seed crowd?
* When you have problems, what should you do?
* How can you be an example to your friends and avoid being seed that doesn't produce?

The Weeds—Who Done It?

"Then the righteous will shine like the sun in their Father's kingdom. Anyone who has ears should listen!" (Matthew 13:43).

This is a story with real drama, mystery, and a wise hero! Once again Jesus takes us to farm country. *"The kingdom of heaven may be compared to a man who sowed good seed in his field"* (Matthew 13:24).

Let me take you back to that time. See if you can picture the quiet farm, perhaps nestled in the green valley of the Jordan River. Look, a farmer guides his oxen as they pull a wooden plow through the soil. Workers follow behind sowing the seed in neat rows. God is good and everybody is happy! (Let's give this good farmer the old Bible name of Nathan.)

After a long hard day, Nathan and his servants head home for a meal that might have included dried fig cakes, roast lamb, grapes, and bread.

But wait, all is not right in the happy land of Galilee. There's a shadowy figure lurking about the place. As the farm lights go off and the farmer sleeps in his bed, evil slips into his field. *"But while people were sleeping, his enemy came, sowed weeds among the wheat, and left"* (Matthew 13:25). I'd call that dastardly,

despicable, dirty, low-down, and nasty. Poor Nathan had no way of knowing trouble was growing in his field. Trouble with a capital WEED.

The wheat sprouted green and strong, but so did the weeds. It didn't seem to take Nathan's servants long to figure out that everything wasn't on the up-and-up. They were puzzled and ran off to tell the boss of their seedy discovery. *"Master, didn't you sow good seed in your field? Then where did the weeds come from?"* (Matthew 13:27). Nathan must have wandered through his fields with a baffled frown. There was only one answer, *"An enemy did this!"* (Matthew 13:28).

Now, Nathan didn't go all crazy. Why? Because he was smart. The servants asked him, *"So, do you want us to go*

TRIVIA

What exactly are oxen? *Very strong but gentle bull-like animals, weighing up to 2,200 pounds.*

and gather them up?" (Matthew 13:28). Remember, when we have big problems, always take them to God in prayer. I'm sure Nathan sat down and prayed to God for an answer. And God came through. Nathan gave his servants these instructions. *"'No,' he said. 'When you gather up the weeds, you might also uproot the wheat with them. Let both grow together until the harvest'"* (Matthew 13:29–30). Now that's an idea that really grows on you!

Harvesttime came and, like many landowners, Nathan may have hired extra workers to cut and store his wheat. To cut the wheat, they used large, curved, wooden or metal

JOKE

What did the oxen say when he finished eating his hay? *"Well, that's the last straw!"*

blades called sickles. I'm sure the harvesters were a little puzzled at Nathan's strange crop of wheat and weeds. He told them, *"Gather the weeds first and tie them in bundles to burn them, but store the wheat in my barn"* (Matthew 13:30). Nathan's patience and wisdom paid off in a successful harvest.

Jesus didn't tell us this story so we could become fabulous farmers. Remember, things are not what they seem in the parables. Like pieces of a puzzle, each person or thing has a special meaning. Let's look at the puzzle piece by piece.

Get ready for the most important part. Jesus is like our friend Nathan who sows good seed. With His hard work, care, and wisdom, the crop grows strong and healthy. Jesus cares for us.

"The field is the world; and the good seed—these are the sons of the kingdom" (Matthew 13:38). Hey, that's us—people who love God and follow Jesus' teachings. Then Jesus said that the harvest-time is the end of the world, and the workers that harvest the wheat are angels. That's what I call real heavenly harvesters!

You may have already guessed that being a weed is not a good thing. *"The weeds are the sons of the evil one, and the enemy who sowed them is the Devil"* (Matthew 13:38–39).

Now that we have all the pieces, what's the big picture? Jesus cares for us! Jesus will send out His angels when the world ends. *"They will gather from His kingdom everything that causes sin and those guilty of lawlessness"* (Matthew 13:41). So evil will be pulled up, cast out, and burned away. See, I told you being a weed was not a good thing!

What about the good seed team? Things are looking very good for the children of God! *"Then the righteous will shine like the sun in their Father's kingdom"* (Matthew 13:43). Now that's the kind of puzzle I like to put together! Sounds like a bright future!

How do we get on the good seed team? Well, that certainly isn't a puzzle. Believe in God and trust Him to forgive your sins. Love God and follow Jesus' teachings. Learn the things that please God, and do them. Hey, that's pretty easy. Everybody can do

TRIVIA

Who was the first person mentioned in the New Testament? *Jesus.*

that! Remember, when troubles pop up in your life, stay calm and look to God for the answers. God will take care of you, just like the wheat in the field. What's your reward for following God? Wow, a bright future in heaven with your Heavenly Father.

QUESTION CORNER

※ What's the reward for doing things God's way?

※ Do you do right things just to get into heaven? Why or why not?

※ When will Jesus come back to harvest His crop?

Mustard Seeds and Yeast, Mighty Small Heroes

"No one should despise your youth; instead you should be an example to the believers in speech, in conduct, in love, in faith, in purity" (1Timothy 4:12).

We can learn a lot from studying even the simplest things in life! Jesus found lessons in the daily activities around Him. He watched what people did—from how they did business together to how they lived at home. He used what He saw and made them into stories. Let's take a look at what's cooking in this parable.

Jesus started this story by saying, *"The kingdom of heaven is like a mustard seed"* (Matthew 13:31). Hold the relish and pass me the ketchup! I didn't even know they had hot dog stands back then! They didn't, but people in Israel have been planting black mustard plants for thousands of years. All to get that tangy mustard powder.

Good things come in small packages, and that's true for the mustard plant. The seed is very tiny—a real garden seed peewee. The mustard's tiny reputation doesn't last long, however, *"but when grown, it's taller than the vegetables and becomes a tree"* (Matthew 13:32). Step back and give this plant some room! The mustard plant can grow to a whopping twelve-feet tall. It becomes the biggest plant in the patch, and *"so . . . the birds of the sky come and nest in its branches"* (Matthew 13:32). Is there something to be learned from this pint-sized-kernel-to-mammoth-mustard-plant success story? A bushel full! More on this spicy story later.

Jesus wasn't finished with his culinary chronicles (that is, cooking tales). *"The kingdom of heaven is like yeast"* (Matthew 13:33). To understand the story of yeast, we have to get even smaller than the mustard seed. Smaller even than this tiny period mark. Yeast is a microscopic marvel that found widespread use in ancient Egypt. They could grow these little one-cell plants on sweet things like sugar. When enough of these

DIDYAKNOW?
Jesus told parables about baking bread with yeast. In one parable, yeast was the hero (Luke 13:20–21), and in the other, yeast was the beast (Luke 12:1).

little funky fungi were grown, bakers throughout the ages added them to their bread dough, like the woman in Jesus' story who mixed it *"into three measures of flour until it spread through all of it"* (Matthew 13:33). Wait just one microscopic second! Fungi in our bread? That's right, thousands of them. Totally unappetizing? Not in the least, or should I say the most?

Once we pop these little fellas into our dough, they begin to produce a gas called carbon dioxide. These fizzy little bubbles of gas get trapped in the dough, making little air pockets. These bubbles make the bread bigger, lighter, and fluffier. Another example of little

TRIVIA

Was bread a main food source for people in the Bible? *Yes.*

self-starters turning into big dynamos!

What do twelve-foot plants and fluffy bread have to do with heaven? To understand that, we have to ask ourselves another question. Did they start out gigantic or fluffy? Nope. They both had starting points—the tiny mustard seed and the even tinier one-celled yeast plant. Our relationship with God also has a starting point. God plants a little seed of love and understanding in our hearts. Each day that we walk with God and learn His teachings, our understanding of Him grows and living His way gets easier.

Like the yeast, God's way of doing things gets worked into our lives. And we discover God's way is always the best way! You could say we rise to God's way of doing things.

We get so excited about the great things God's doing in our lives that we can't help but tell other people. Our love for God just sort of bubbles over into all areas of our lives. It doesn't take long before doing things God's way is the only comfortable way of living.

We are so happy people want to be around us—just like the birds in the mustard plant. People want to know how we got so happy and how they can get happy too. What happens next is really amazing! God plants a little seed inside that person's heart too.

How can we help God plant His love? Simply turn life's situations into godly opportunities! If a friend has said something or done something to hurt your feelings—show God's love by forgiving them. Take time out to do things for other people, like helping a neighbor kid fix his bike, or baking cookies for a sick friend. When they wonder why, just tell them what God has done for you. It's the little everyday things that really display God's love in our hearts and make a BIG difference in people's lives. People will wonder how a little person like you got such a giant-sized heart!

When you encounter life's big and small circumstances, have the attitudes that God admires, like thankfulness, forgiveness, kindness, faithfulness, honesty, and charity. They might be tough at first, but those little right choices turn you into a strong person who lives for God.

JOKE

Why is yeast a bad mathematician? *Because it multiplies by dividing.*

And that's a recipe for a successful life!
Small changes make for BIG results!

QUESTION CORNER

* What other ways can you show
  God's love in your life?
* What can you say when a friend asks
  you about God? If you don't
  know, how can you find out?
* What small seeds are growing in
  your life?
* Were you ever in a situation when
  you started out with a bad attitude
  and then chose to have a good
  one? What happened?

Treasure Stories

"For where your treasure is, there your heart will be also" (Matthew 6:21).

Do you find the thought of buried treasure exciting? Jesus told the stories of two separate men who discovered riches in the most interesting places.

Jesus didn't tell us very much about the first man. Maybe, for our purposes, he can be a shepherd tending his sheep. Let's imagine he was. Can you picture the first light of morning just peeking over the hills surrounding the city of Jerusalem? A shepherd (he might have had a name like Elam) had just discovered that one of his sheep strayed in the night. Elam walked far in search of it, but still couldn't find the stray. Suddenly he saw something really amazing peeking out of the dirt in a field.

Jesus doesn't tell us what the treasure was, but if we look back at what sorts of things people valued in those days, we can make a guess. Maybe Elam found something like copper ore—rocks with specks of copper in them. Copper ore has a beautiful bright-green weathered color that might have attracted his attention.

The golden-red, shiny metal called copper has been used for thousands of years. People mined it out of the earth and made coins, cooking utensils, huge pots, and jewelry out of it. If he discovered copper—what a find!

Quickly he covered his new discovery with dirt and reburied it. Maybe he ran back to his sheep and excitedly ordered his son to help herd the flock to the market in Jerusalem. *"Then in his joy he goes and sells everything he has"* (Matthew 13:44). With the money he raised from selling his sheep, he bought the field and all that was in it. Last seen, our ex-shepherd was rich from his copper, and was a happy man as he searched for more treasure in his special field.

The second man Jesus tells us about was *"a merchant"* (Matthew 13:45). What's a merchant? I'm glad you

JOKE

Where do Eskimos keep their money? *In snow banks.*

asked! A merchant is a person who buys and sells any variety of goods.

Now, come with me to the busiest place in the entire kingdom. Pass through the gates of Jerusalem and enter the wonders of the marketplace. It was a dazzling place of fascinating sights and sounds—exotic perfumes, brightly colored fabrics, and shiny bronze and copper containers. Shopkeepers haggled and laughed with their many customers.

In the middle of this lively market was our merchant. What was he looking for? Something very special, something very rare, something very beautiful! *"Again, the kingdom of heaven is like a merchant in search of fine pearls"* (Matthew 13:45).

He slipped into the shade of a shop and found the most perfect pearl he had ever seen! It seemed to glow! But he didn't have enough coins to buy this treasure. *"He went and sold everything he had"* (Matthew 13:46). Does this sound familiar? It should. What did he do next? One guess per customer only! If you guessed, *"bought it"* (Matthew 13:46), you'd be right!

Okay, smart guys, what did we learn? Both men found treasure beyond their wildest dreams. Both men sold all that they had to get that treasure. Now, what do you think is the biggest treasure in the entire universe? It isn't billions of dollars, a mountain of diamonds, or even an ocean of pearls. Heaven is the

---

TRIVIA

What did the man say when he walked into a store? *"Ouch!"*

---

brightest and best treasure of all!

How exactly do we find heaven? It isn't sticking out of the ground or on sale at the mall. When we seek God and follow Jesus, we are given the map to life's true treasure. What's on that map? God's directions for having a good life. The Bible is the map we need to read!

Remember, both the shepherd and the merchant gave up all they had to gain their treasure. They sold it all to get it all. And God's kingdom is the best treasure of all. We have to do the same. We have to give up our own way of doing things, our own desires, and our own choices. We have to let God's will be our will. It WILL take a huge step of faith! The merchant and shepherd had to trust God to keep their treasures safe for them until they could claim them.

The moment the shepherd found the treasure and the merchant found the pearl, they had to make a decision. The shepherd could have gone back to herding his sheep, and the merchant could have gone off to find a less expensive pearl. We all have to decide if we want to follow Jesus and make Him our personal Savior, or go our own way. That choice is the first step on the road to what God treasures. Part of God's gift to us is a life full of love, friends, joy, peace, and success! When we give our lives back to God, we discover that God gives us back a better life. Now that's the type of exchange I like to make! We can never match God's

DIDYAKNOW?

One of the largest pearls ever found weighed over 14 pounds!

generosity, but we can thank Him with an obedient heart. Remember, God takes care of us because we are like precious treasure to Him. His love is a gift for life! There is nothing hidden about that!

QUESTION CORNER

☀ When Jesus talks about treasure, what is He talking about?
☀ What types of things do you give up when you follow Jesus?
☀ What do you gain by following Jesus?

Seventy-seven Times

"Be kind and compassionate to one another, forgiving one another, just as God also forgave you in Christ" (Ephesians 4:32).

Seventy-seven times was the answer. Do you want to know the question? *"Then Peter came to [Jesus] and said, 'Lord, how many times could my brother sin against me and I forgive him? As many as seven times?'"* (Matthew 18:21). Often when Jesus was asked a question, He answered with a story. The parable of the unforgiving servant is part of Jesus' answer to Peter's important question.

A generous king had lent his servants money. Time passed, and the king decided that it was time to talk with each of his servants about how much they owed and if they could pay him back. *"One who owed ten thousand talents was brought before him"* (Matthew 18:24). Just one talent was a huge chunk of money, probably thousands of dollars. So, a man who owed ten thousand talents was in big-time debt and in big-time trouble. Let's give this man the old Bible name of Azel. So our friend Azel owed the king millions of dollars, but he couldn't repay the king. Now the king wasn't a bad fellow, but he was at his wits' end as to what to do with his servant. The king was very

upset with Azel and *"commanded that he, his wife, his children, and everything he had be sold to pay the debt"* (Matthew 18:25). Harsh as it may sound, it was common practice in those times.

Azel fell on his knees before the king. *"Be patient with me, and I will pay you everything!"* (Matthew 18:26). The king was a very, very kind man. He *"had compassion, released him, and forgave him the loan"* (Matthew 18:27). Azel must have been surprised! He was free! His family was free! The king had forgiven him his debt of millions! Now he owed absolutely nothing! It seemed like a miracle! It *was* a miracle! Yippee! Azel left the throne room a very happy man.

Leaving the palace, Jesus said, Azel met one of his fellow servants. It just so happened that this fellow owed

TRIVIA

What did Jesus say we should do with our enemies? *Love them.*

Azel money. A hundred denarii to be exact. That would have been around three or four months' wages. Certainly not nearly as much as Azel's own million-dollar debt. What do you think Azel did? If you said, "Forgave him," you're kinder than Azel. No. It seems our friend Azel had a very short memory. Surprisingly short! He grabbed his fellow servant and actually began to choke him!

"'Pay what you owe!' At this, his fellow slave fell down and began begging him, 'Be patient with me, and I will pay you back'" (Matthew 18:28–29). I don't know about you, but this sounds very familiar to me. What do you think happened next?

Wrong again! Azel refused to forgive the man his debt. *"He wasn't willing. On the contrary, he went and threw him into prison until he could pay what was owed"* (Matthew 18:30).

Well, the palace was a busy place with lots of people in it. *"When the other slaves saw what had taken place, they were deeply distressed and went and reported to their master everything that had happened"* (Matthew 18:31). The king listened to what they said and then asked for Azel to be sent to him.

Azel was brought before the king. The king probably stared at him for a long time before speaking. *"You wicked slave! I forgave you all that debt because you begged me. Shouldn't you also have had mercy on your fellow slave, as I had mercy on you?"* (Matthew 18:32–33). The king was so angry that he turned foolish Azel over to the jailers until Azel could pay back all that he owed.

Jesus ended this story with this warning, *"So will My heavenly Father also do to you if each of you does not forgive his brother from his heart"* (Matthew 18:35).

In other words, if you want to be forgiven, then forgiving others should be your first order of the day. So, the next time someone does something hurtful to you and asks for your forgiveness, don't be an Azel. Answer the way Jesus answers us! "I forgive you not one time, not seven times, but seventy-seven times and more!"

God's mercy has changed people's lives. Mercy is an unlimited commodity. We can never have too much! Our forgiveness is a wonderful gift we need to give to one another. It melts away people's hurt feelings, anger, and fear. Mercy can be the foundation of trust and friendship between people and even nations. If we are happy to receive God's forgiveness, then we must never forget to forgive others. God loves a forgiving heart! If you need help to really forgive someone, just pray and God will help you. And it doesn't really matter if they accept your forgiveness, because God knows you took that extra step to be kind and loving. My motto is "FORGIVENESS. DON'T LEAVE HOME WITHOUT IT!"

Do try this at home! When you

DIDYAKNOW?

A very good day's wages in Jesus' time was one Roman silver coin.

43

get angry with someone—stop and take a "mercy moment." Take a deep breath, count to ten or seventy-seven if you need to, and then try to work things out with that person. Perhaps, after thinking about it, you may even find you want to say you're sorry or accept their apology. Take time to talk and work things out so both of you are happy again. Just remember, forgiveness isn't a sometimes thing. It needs to be an every time thing.

QUESTION CORNER

* How did you feel when someone forgave you?
* What should Azel have done and why?
* Is there anyone you need to forgive? When and how will you do that?

To Do or Not to Do?

"Whatever you do, do it enthusiastically, as something done for the Lord and not for men" (Colossians 3:23).

This is a story about attitudes and actions. We all have different attitudes at different times. An attitude is the way we do things, and also the *reason* we do things. Let me give you an example. Suppose you are in a bad mood because you have to clean your room, but you clean your room anyway because it is your responsibility. It's the old "I'll do it, but I don't have to like it" attitude. Sometimes actions and attitudes get all mixed up and confusing. Read this parable and you'll find out why.

There was a father who had two sons. He went to his first son and said, *"My son, go, work in the vineyard today"* (Matthew 21:28). Well, cancel the donkey races and all the other really fun stuff he had planned! Dad wants him to work.

JOKE

Why couldn't the grape finish the race? *It ran out of juice.*

Now, you might need some extra info to help you get the picture. A vineyard was usually a balcony-like garden cut into the side of a sunny hillside. This was a special place because it was where the family grew their grapevines. Grapes were a very important crop in Jesus' time. Working in the vineyard was hard and time consuming. You had to repair the garden's stone walls, weed around the vines, prune the branches, plant new vines, build wood supports so that grapes didn't rot or fall to the ground, and kill the small rodents that tunneled into the garden to eat the grapes. Sometimes you even had to spend long hours in the watchtower guarding the vines against hungry herd animals and thieving people. Talk about your full job jar!

The first son thought about all that hard work. Maybe hanging out at the watchtower or killing small, incredibly fast mammals didn't appeal to him that day. Or maybe he had a prime donkey in today's race. At any rate, *"he answered, 'I don't want to!'"* (Matthew 21:29). Well, that's an attitude of the not-so-great kind. He had a mood as

unpleasant as . . . well . . . sour grapes! But, later he thought about it, changed his mind and went to the vineyard to work. Jesus didn't say why the sudden switch in plans (maybe the donkey was dozy or went lame), but soon the son was off gardening with gusto. He was doing his all for good ol' Dad!

His father didn't know about his change of heart, so he went and asked his second son the same thing. This time the father was probably pleased with his younger son's response, *"I will, sir"* (Matthew 21:30). What a great answer!

TRIVIA

In Bible times what did they do with the grapes they grew? *They ate them fresh, dried them to make raisin clusters, or squeezed them to make wine.*

This is more like it! He even said "Sir"! How polite, how nice, how obedient—and how wrong! Later the second son thought about all that hard work, and even though he said yes—*"he didn't go"* (Matthew 21:30). He certainly started out strong with the right attitude, but then his actions didn't follow through. Again, we are left to guess at the reason for this lack of promised action. Maybe all his buddies were at those donkey races, and it was just too much fun to resist!

Which of the two sons did what his father wanted? The first son! A case of the three AAAs—Attitude, Adjustment, and Action. His attitude may have been wrong to start out with, but with a little adjustment he changed his mind, and his actions were obedient in the end. He did the work—unlike his brother, who talked a good talk, but in the end did a big zero worth of work.

Okay, before you get all happy and pleased as grape punch that your parents don't have a vineyard tucked in the corner of your yard, you're not off the hook! Our belief in God can be just like the two sons. Some people say they believe in God, but their actions just don't show it. They talk a good talk and are very polite, but they don't do the things God wants them to do. Others may have started out not following God's teachings, but they changed their minds and put their faith into action by doing the things God wants them to do. Which is better? You got it! We need to honor God by both saying and doing His will. Saying we will is just not enough—we have to DO it.

You can put those right attitudes into high performance in your daily activities and life. Remember, in everything you do, do it like you were doing it for God. Why? Because you are! If you agreed to deliver newspapers every morning at 5 o'clock—wake up, early bird, and hit the road. If your parents trust you to take care of your pet every day—get out the dog brush and pour those doggie num-nums. Show the people that care about you that you can put into action what you promise. If you say you will do something, you do it.

God wants us to be people who can be relied upon and trusted. So, get

> **TRIVIA**
> Who was the first man to plant a vineyard? *Noah.*

out there and get those right attitudes into incredible godly action! The answer to the age-old question, "To do or not to do?" is do it and do it well! Hey, well done! And that shouldn't be a rare thing!

QUESTION CORNER

☀ Do you always try to do what you say you will? Why or why not?

☀ Has someone ever let you down? How did it make you feel?

☀ Why does life seem to work out better when you are obedient to God? (Sssh, here's a hint: He designed the world.)

Villains in the Vines

"Instruct them to do good, to be rich in good works, to be generous, willing to share" (1 Timothy 6:18).

This parable has action and danger. In fact, some of the people in this story are just about as mean as a bulldog with his collar on too tight, and as bad-tempered as a wasp caught in a soda bottle. I think you get the gener-al idea. This is how the story goes. (I'll summarize parts of it for you.)

"There was a man, a landowner, who planted a vineyard, put a fence around it, dug a winepress in it, and built a watchtower" (Matthew 21:33). Talk about your

home improvements!

"He leased it to tenant farmers and went away" (Matthew 21:33). It was a very common practice in those days for a wealthy landowner to go away and leave his land in the care of renting farmers who grew and harvested the crops. The landowner would, of course, get a large share of the crop that was grown. You could call him a shareholder!

When harvest time approached, Jesus tells how our landowner sent three of his servants to collect his share of the fruit. What happened next was just terrible! The renting farmers attacked those poor servants! The farmers beat them up! The farmers threw stones at them. How rude! In general, they did some pretty nasty stuff. One poor fellow was even killed.

As you can imagine, this didn't make the landowner very happy. Jesus said the landowner decided to send an entire squad of servants out to the vineyard. The renting farmers attacked those servants as well! Now, this was getting way out of hand. What to do next? Ah, the landowner had an idea. *"Finally, he sent his son to them. 'They will respect my son,' he said"* (Matthew 21:37).

A big "uh-oh" on that idea too. *"When the tenant farmers saw the son, they said among themselves, 'This is the heir. Come, let's kill him and seize his inheritance!' So they seized him and threw him out of the vineyard, and killed him"* (Matthew 21:38–39). The farmers

JOKE

What did the grapevine say to the grape thief?

"Leaf me alone."

weren't doing a whole lot of intelligent thinking in this story. Killing the landowner's son wasn't going to buy them the farm, so to speak. I mean, what did they expect? Did they think the landowner would say, "Oh, my! Silly me. Of course they should have the farm. That would be a good reward for killing my son"? Wrong! They got into big trouble, and rightly so.

What do you think the landowner will do to those villainous vine growers? *"He will destroy those terrible men in a terrible way . . . and lease his vineyard to other farmers who will give him his produce at the harvest"* (Matthew 21:41).

DIDYAKNOW?

Today wine is stored in fancy glass bottles. In Jesus' time, wine was stored in clay jars or skin bags.

As you might have noticed, there were no happy endings in this story. The poor landowner lost his son, and the farmers got punished for their foolish, wicked ways. Jesus had this to say about the story. *"Therefore I tell you, the kingdom of God will be taken away from you and given to a nation producing its fruit"* (Matthew 21:43).

Now this parable has a double whammy in it. Remember how things in parables aren't what they seem? Well, here the landowner's servants were like God's messengers coming to tell God's people that they had to do things God's way. But no one was listening. And who was the son? You got it! Jesus. He was predicting His own death and showing people's attitudes: "Get rid of Jesus and our way will work best." Ever heard something like that? "I don't have to do things God's way. I can do what I want." Uh-oh. Wrong! Big mistake! Huge! God will take away His "land"—His kingdom and blessings—from people with that attitude and give it to others who will do things His way.

So which do you want to be? Good choice.

That's the first whammy. Here's the second. It was painfully clear that the farmers had forgotten that the land they worked was not their own. The land, buildings, grapes, vines, winepress, watchtower, and absolutely everything in the garden belonged to the master of the garden. (Hold all our stuff and mark it "return to owner!")

Are we just as forgetful? Whose garden are we living and working in?

The world is God's garden! But I'll tell you a secret—we don't even have to rent it. God has given it to us for free. But, (and this is important,) are we taking God's generosity, kindness, and forgiveness for granted? Are we strutting around like WE'RE the masters? If we have to ask, "Who's the boss around here?" we're already on the road to big trouble. God's the boss! No ifs, ands, or buts about it.

Where we live—our home, our possessions, and the things we enjoy— are all gifts from God! We are free to enjoy them, but we shouldn't forget to always be thankful for them. When God comes knocking on your door—be ready

TRIVIA

Which is more blessed to God, to give or to receive? *To give.*

to share His harvest.

We can do this by helping the needy in our own city, financially supporting mission work in other countries, or just spending time with people who might need a helping hand. You look like a pretty handy person to me! There are a hundred ways you can spread God's harvest around. Maybe you could make a weekly visit to a seniors' home to talk, play games, or read to new friends. Or you could baby-sit for free once a week for a single mother so she can go out. With your parents' help, find out about groups at church that could use your special talents. If we don't share our blessings with others, God will give His harvest to someone who will.

Spreading God's love and generosity around is our way of giving back to God His share of the harvest. It is also our way of thanking God for His gifts, love, forgiveness, and for giving us His Son, Jesus. Being God's good tenant is all in a day's work!

QUESTION CORNER

* Make a list of all the good things God has given you.
* What are some ways that you can share God's generosity with others?
* Why is God so giving to you if you don't deserve it?

And a Whole Lot More

"**Be strong and courageous. Don't be afraid or be terrified, because the Lord your God is with you everywhere you go**" (Joshua 1:9).

This is a story about people who have what it takes, who are on the ball, willing to give it their best shot, put their hearts into it, and do it right. This is a parable about three different servants.

Jesus told of a well-to-do man who was going on a journey. He called his three servants to him. (Jesus didn't name them but let's call them Sam, Matt, and Ben—all fairly common names in the Bible.) *To one he gave five talents [of money]; to another two; and to another, one—to each according to his own ability. Then he went on a journey"* (Matthew 25:15).

A talent is a sum of money that would be equal to, say, several thousand dollars. The master expected the servants to use his money wisely while he was away. Let's find out if these guys had a "talent" for money handling.

Sam was given five talents. That was a huge responsibility, but Sam was up to the challenge. He probably did his homework on businesses around town.

He may have invested his money with a farmer, or perhaps a craftsman. Investing means he likely gave those businesses money to buy seed, or purchase raw metal, stone, or leathers to make their goods. When the crop was harvested or the products sold, Sam would be paid a percentage of the profits, and so he would make more money. Pretty smart guy, that Sam. Whatever he did, he *"put them to work, and earned five more"* (Matthew 25:16).

Matt was no slouch with a buck either. *"In the same way the man with two earned two more"* (Matthew 25:17).

But what can we say about Ben, the third servant? It seems that responsibility just made him nervous and worried. What if he invested the money unwisely and lost the one talent

the master had given him? What to do; WHAT to do? Aha! Or should I say, "Oh no!" *"The man who had received one talent went off, dug a hole in the ground, and hid his master's money"* (Matthew 25:18). Not exactly a smart business-person's scheme, if you ask my opinion. But who's asking?

"After a long time the master of those slaves came and settled accounts with them" (Matthew 25:19). Sam stepped forward. *"Master, you gave me five talents. Look, I've earned five more talents"* (Matthew 25:20).

His master was very impressed! *"Well done, good and faithful slave! You were faithful over a few things; I will put you in charge of many things. Enter your master's joy!"* (Matthew 25:21). Talk about a prompt promotion!

Matt had doubled his master's money. Again the master was happy. Matt's responsibility around the place was also increased.

At this point I think Ben realized too late that he hadn't exactly made the perfect executive decision (that's boss language for choice). As he handed over the same amount that was given to him, he explained, *"Master, I know you. You're a difficult man, reaping where you haven't sown and gathering where you haven't scattered seed. So I was afraid and went off and hid your talent in the ground. Look, you have what is yours"* (Matthew 25:24–25).

To say his master was under-whelmed is an understatement. *"You evil, lazy slave! . . . You should have deposited my money with the bankers. And when I returned I would have received my money back with interest"* (Matthew 25:26–27). At least the bank would have paid the master a little money for the temporary USE of his money.

The master, in his anger and disgust, took the money from bumbling Ben and gave it to smart Sam. Ben was sent away from the house, and DID NOT share in his master's happiness.

You don't have to be a financial whiz to benefit from this story. In fact, let's update the meaning of the talents. God blesses us with so many things like different abilities or "talents"—you can be good at math, singing, writing, cooking, computers, art, science . . . the list can go on, and on, and on. The important thing is not what you're good at, but whether you are using those talents the way God wants you to! Are you like Sam and showing your stuff, or are you like Ben, hiding your gifts? ALWAYS REMEMBER that God gave you a talent to use. He wants you to be successful! Do everything with all your heart and ability, and God will give you more talents and skills. Just like the master in the story! But it is up to you to put away your fears, have faith in God, and have confidence. That type of confidence earned Matt and Sam more!

JOKE

A lazy gardener asked his boss for a letter of recommendation. The boss wrote three pages of things the gardener could do. At the bottom he added, "But he *won't!*"

If you don't use it, you'll lose it just like poor Ben. Talk about a real loser!

So, when your teacher asks you to sing the lead in the choir, or do a project for the science fair, don't say NO! Say Y-E-S! Make the most of that opportunity! God will continue to open those doors and unlock those marvelous talents! God wants to share in your success and happiness because He's your biggest fan!

QUESTION CORNER

* What talents do you think God has given you?
* When you are nervous, what should you do?
* How can you use your talents to "get more"?

The Seeds of Mystery

"The Lord will always guide you, and will satisfy your needs in dry places, and make your bones strong. You will be like a watered garden, and like a spring of water whose waters never run dry" (Isaiah 58:11).

This story is so *deep* I think you're going to really *dig* it. Trust me, it will *grow* on you. Here's the parable of the "secret seed" if you really want to *stick* it out. Get it? Dig, plant, grow, stick! Okay, okay, I'll stop already.

Here's the story!

"A man scatters seed on the ground" (Mark 4:26). Have you ever thought about what a seed is? It's a little package with big potential—that's what it is. In that tiny little speck of hard shell is the

DNA or blueprint for an entire plant from a giant redwood tree towering hundreds of feet in the air to an itty-bitty flower. They all start out as seeds. There's a whole lot of stuff packed in those little fellas! Kind of like me!

Roll over, Fido; seeds make the perfect pet! Okay, I admit you can't teach them to fetch, but you don't have to take them for walks either. The point is—once planted, a seed pretty much does its own thing. It starts to form little baby roots, then little by little a sprout begins to push its way through the dirt to the surface until a seedling begins to unfold its leaves and grow into an adult plant. You can't teach a seed this. Nope, it just does what comes naturally. A little self-starting phenomenon! In our story all that the farmer can do is wait for that natural miracle to happen. *"Night and day he sleeps and gets up, and the seed sprouts and grows—he doesn't know how"* (Mark 4:27).

God designed a seed to follow a perfect pattern of growth. God also provides the proper ingredients to help it grow: water, air, sunlight, and good soil, full of minerals. *"The soil produces a crop by itself—first the blade, then the head, and then the ripe grain on the head"* (Mark 4:28). Inch by inch, day by day, the farmer's field begins to grow and mature.

It is such an amazing and satisfying sight to see a field of golden wheat rippling in the wind just waiting to be

harvested. (Hey, I know about farms! Last year I was the narrator for "Farms Are Us.") Anyway, trust me, a ripe field is a gift from God! Up to this point the seed and soil have done all the work. Now it is time for the farmer to do his job. *"As soon as the crop is ready, he sends for the sickle, because harvest has come"* (Mark 4:29). All the farmer's watchful patience has paid off with carts full of grain heading to the threshing floor. On the threshing floor the wheat kernels are separated from the stalks, and the farmer's job is done. Give those oxen an extra helping of straw, and sit back and relax!

DIDYAKNOW?

Four common garden plants eaten in ancient Israel were melons, cucumbers, onions, and garlic.

We talked about God planting a seed in our hearts before. Let's look at this process a little closer. God will put a little seed of love for and understanding of Him in each of us. Then He will put us in an environment that will help that seed grow. Just like a seed, He gives us all the elements that we need to grow as Christians. He gives us people who care about us—like loving parents, grandparents, aunts and uncles, and friends.

God also gives us people who can help us learn even more about Him—like Sunday school teachers, ministers, or youth group leaders. They teach us the right way to grow with God. With all this care and attention, God's seed grows and fills our hearts, minds, and souls. Hey, that's a good thing. He gives us the Bible so we can learn more about

Him and His ways.

That's what God does for us. What can we do for Him? We have to choose to follow God's Word always and obey His laws. That's not hard at all! Just like the seed, it becomes a natural way of being! Now that's really supernatural! When that seed is finally fully grown, watch out! We become strong people in God, ready to do the things He wants us to do. We become God's mature harvest!

Sure, we get tons of support from our family, friends, and church, but we also have a responsibility to help our own relationship with God grow. We need to spend quiet time with God, pray, read the Bible, follow God's teachings, and get involved in activities at our church. If we have some questions about God or the Bible, we should take the time to talk to our parents, minister, or teachers. The more you learn about God—the more you want to learn! That's what I call putting your roots deep in the life God has for you. When you do, you become stronger and stronger, and become the person God wants you to be. Just like the farmer was rewarded with a successful harvest—you are rewarded with a phenomenal life! A life full of good friends, good experiences at home or school, and exciting things to see and do. All because you live your life the way God designed it. Just like He designed the flower to be

DIDYAKNOW?

The largest seed in the world is from the giant fan palm. It can weigh up to 44 pounds.

beautiful and the redwood tree to be gigantic, God has a blueprint for your life. It doesn't have to be a mystery if you follow His directions!

QUESTION CORNER

- How can you fill yourself up with God's good stuff so you grow strong?
- What can you dig your roots into?
- If a friend has questions about God, would you know how to help him or her find the answers?
- Is there an area in your life that you want to see grow in God's direction? Why? How can you do that?

Forgiveness for Free

"Anyone who hides his sin will not prosper, but anyone who confesses and forsakes it will receive mercy" (Proverbs 28:13).

We all make mistakes, big and small. We can try as hard as we can to avoid them, but they still happen. How we handle them is the key. This parable about two men with big worries will shed some light on our misdeeds and God's kindness.

"A creditor had two debtors" (Luke 7:41). Let's give these two hardworking guys the names Pete and Zack. Now, I know that in those days it certainly wasn't easy making a living. For some people, like

small farm owners, life was a hard road caught between hefty taxes and the high cost of keeping a farm running. Often, even good farmers ran into big-time debt. Sometimes they would seek the help of a moneylender. Like our modern day banks, these lenders would loan the farmer money to cover his taxes or keep the farm going. The farmer hoped that after a good harvest he could pay the moneylender back. Zack and Pete went to a guy fondly known around town as, let's say, "Lenny the Lender."

Unfortunately, sometimes the harvest wasn't good, and the farmer found

TRIVIA

Which items were once used as money: shells, stones, leather, metals, spices, feathers, or rare woods? *All of them have been used as money.*

himself in money troubles. Perhaps Pete and Zack in our story found themselves in JUST such a problem with our friend Lenny. *"One owed five hundred denarii, and the other fifty"* (Luke 7:41). A denarii was a Roman silver coin. Zack, you could say, was in a sackful of trouble. A silver denarii was worth about one day's wage. He owed Lenny over a year's worth of work, including holidays and weekends. It was going to take Zack a long, long time to repay his debt—perhaps years. He was clearly way over his head in money troubles. Pete was only about knee-deep in his troubles. Perhaps with hard work and careful planning he could wade out of his debt in just a year or two. That is, if Lenny the Lender would wait that long.

Lenny could do a number of things to get his money back. Which "door" will

he choose? Behind **Door Number One**—Lenny could force the men to sell their farms and all they owned. **Door Number Two**—Lenny could even sell Zack and Pete's families into slavery to pay back their debts. **Door Number Three**—Lenny could send the men to prison for years.

Slavery or prison didn't seem like very nice prizes. I'm sure the two men were very frightened by the unhappy consequences of their money troubles. What did Lenny do? Ah, but wait! Yes! There is a **Door Number Four!**

Lenny showed the contestants—I mean borrowers—what is behind that fourth and last door! *"He graciously forgave them both"* (Luke 7:42). Wow, Lenny

the Lender, what a great, great guy! He was generous and kind to both Pete and Zack! What a relief! No worries, no debt, no prison, no slavery! Zack and Pete were delirious with gratitude. As they walked through town, they were laughing, dancing, jumping for joy, and singing at the top of their lungs—and all at the same time, if you can believe it! They were a two-man parade!

Jesus asked this question of His host Simon (He was at a dinner party), *"So, which of them will love him more?"* (Luke 7:42). Do you know? Take a guess!

"Simon answered, 'I suppose the one he forgave more.'

"'You have judged correctly,' He told him" (Luke 7:43). Well, give Simon a big prize for that smart answer!

God can change our lives for the

better no matter what kind of trouble we find ourselves in. In fact, we all make mistakes sometimes. Why? Because we aren't perfect and never can be—no matter how hard we try. God is the only one who is truly perfect. Jesus compared our mistakes or sins to the money owed by our two friends. Who is more grateful to God, a person who has made many wrong choices and mistakes in his life and has been forgiven by God, or the person who only sinned just a little? The first person, right? God has forgiven him more!

How we handle our sins or mistakes is important. We can't just sweep them under the rug and hope that God won't notice. God checks under our spiritual rug. We should always bring our sins to God and ask for His forgiveness. Big or small, if we believe in Him, God will forgive our sins because He loves us ALL the time.

Do we stop there? Nope, our job is only half done. We have to ask God to help us learn from our mistakes, give us the strength to correct them, and learn how to avoid doing them again. Then we go on from there with a clean conscience and a healthier walk with God.

JOKE

Why did the baker go to the bank?

He kneaded the dough.

Facing your mistakes isn't easy, and sometimes we try to ignore them or pretend that they don't exist. Mistakes don't go away. Have you ever tried to hide a mistake or even tried to fix it yourself so nobody would notice? Say you broke your mom's favorite vase playing ball in the living room. You knew it was wrong to play there, but you got carried away. And then it was a sad case of toss, crash, smash, and groan. Hiding the vase would have been a temporary solution, and trying to fix it yourself wouldn't have worked—unless you were great at gluing two million microscopic ceramic pieces together. Let's face it, brain surgery would have been easier. You just had to tell your mom and face the consequences. Admit you were wrong, apologize, and ask for her forgiveness.

To your surprise your very cool mom appreciated that you were honest and knew that you learned a valuable lesson. She forgave you. How did your mom learn to be so cool? She learned all her great mom stuff from her heavenly Father!

Don't try to solve your big and small mistakes on your own. You please God by trusting Him to help you do things His way. Remember, always work out your mistakes or sins with God, and He'll guide you on how to deal with the rest! And don't forget to be as forgiving of others as God is of you! Mistakes might happen, but forgiveness is always available!

QUESTION CORNER

- Have you done anything God won't forgive you for? Why or why not?
- How did God's forgiveness make you feel?
- What will be your response when someone asks for your forgiveness?

Two Goofs and a Good Guy

"See to it that no one repays evil for evil to anyone, but always pursue what is good for one another and for all" (1 Thessalonians 5:15).

Aloha, bonjour, guten tag, ihola, konnichi-wa, and hello! These are just a few of the ways people around the world say, "Hi-there, nice to meet ya!" It's just part of being neighborly. Who exactly are our neighbors? Easy, the people who live in the house right next door! Right? For me that would be the next book on the shelf. That's true, but maybe we have to go a little further than that to find God's answer.

"An expert in the law stood up to test [Jesus], saying. 'Teacher, what must I do to inherit eternal life?'

"'What is written in the law?' He asked him. 'How do you read it?'

"He answered:

'You shall love the Lord your God with all your heart, with all your soul, with all your strength, and with all your mind; and your neighbor as yourself'" (Luke 10:25–27).

Good question and answer, but the wrong attitude. Remember this expert was testing Jesus. He then asked this question: *"And who is my neighbor?"* (Luke 10:29). Ask Jesus an important question and He'll give you an impressive answer. Here's His answering parable.

Picture a single traveler journeying down a lonely stretch of dirt road heading toward the ancient farming city of Jericho. Let's give him the name of Ammiel.

"A man was going down from Jerusalem to Jericho and fell into the hands of robbers. They stripped him, beat him up, and fled, leaving him half dead. A priest happened to be going down that road" (Luke 10:30–31). A priest was God's representative and the protector of the Law in Israel. He would be something like the minister of your church. Wow, how great and how timely! If anybody was going to give our poor beat-up Ammiel a helping hand, you'd think this would be THE MAN. But, don't expect a 911 call

JOKE

Knock! Knock!
Who's there?
Sarah. *Sarah who?* Sarah a doctor in the house?

just yet—even if they had them back then. *"When he saw him, he passed by on the other side"* (Luke 10:31). Hold the phone! (I told you not to expect that call.) That's not what he's supposed to do! But he slipped on by anyway.

The next traveler who came down the road was a Levite. Nope, that has nothing to do with the kind of pants he wore. A Levite was a priest's assistant. He'd be like an elder in your church, or maybe a member of the prayer team. I mean, here's a fellow with "hero" written all over him! The Levite spotted our victim and *"passed by on the other side"* (Luke 10:32). What? What does a guy have to do to get a little help around here?

JOKE

What people travel the fastest?

Russians.

Then a Samaritan came along. This man lived in a city called Samaria that overlooked the main road to Jerusalem. We can give him the name of Sam. Works for me! Being neighbors, you would think the two cities were on friendly terms. Unfortunately the citizens of these two cities didn't like each other and did not get along—at all. Samaritans were only half Jewish, and that caused some hard feelings on both sides.

It seemed unlikely that this man would want to help a traveler from Jerusalem. Oh, contraire, my doubting friends. (What I mean is: wrong!) Jesus said Sam saw the wounded man and *"he had compassion. He went over to him and bandaged his wounds, pouring on oil and wine. Then he put him on his own animal, brought him to an inn, and took care of him. The next day he took out two denarii, gave them to the innkeeper, and said, 'Take care of him; and when I come back I'll reimburse you for whatever extra you spend'* (Luke 10:33–35). Talk about the full meal deal! Would you help a guy who thought you were no good? Well, Sam was quite a stand-up guy—a humanitarian with the most! Yes, we have finally found our hero in the most unlikely person!

Jesus asked the Law expert this question, *"'Which of these three do you think proved to be a neighbor to the man who fell into the hands of the robbers?'*

[The Law expert answered] *"'The one who showed mercy to him.'*

"Then Jesus told him, 'Go and do the same'" (Luke 10:36–37).

Who are our neighbors? We can find neighbors anywhere, whether we are in our own town or traveling far. We are to follow the example of good ol' Sam by striving to do good wherever and whenever we can. Why, just the other week I helped the narrator in the next book make her conclusions! That's an all-day job! Anyway, being a good neighbor means keeping an eye open for ways to be kind and helpful to the people around us, no matter who they are.

There are a hundred little ways each day for you to be a Samaritan hero: give up your seat on the bus for that elderly person, or offer part of

DIDYAKNOW?

Jericho is about 800 feet below sea level, making it one of the lowest cities in the world.

your lunch to a classmate you don't get along with. You need to share God's kindness with everybody, no matter who they are. Make the most out of those "neighborly" opportunities! You can be a standup example of God's love on earth. When you do, you'll discover new neighbors have a way of turning into lifetime friends.

QUESTION CORNER

☀ What types of things can you do for someone in need? Like who?

☀ How do you know when to be a good Samaritan? Were you ever a good Sam to someone? What happened? How did you feel afterward?

☀ Has anybody helped you in times of trouble? How did it make you feel?

Foolishly Rich

"Honor the Lord with your money and the first part of your income. Then your storehouses will be filled seven times over, and your wine vats will overflow with new wine" (Proverbs 3:9–10).

Watch out! Be on your guard! Greed, envy, dissatisfaction, and pride are attitudes that can become a big part of the way you live your life—if you're not careful. Once you invite them into your home, you'll need more than a pest-control guy to get them out. You'll need godly control!

One day a man asked Jesus for help. It seems he and his brother were having a hard time deciding how to divide the home, land, and belongings their father left them. Ah, an important opportunity for a positively, perfect parable to explain God's heart. In other words—Jesus told this story.

There was a very successful and rich farmer. We could call him Immer. Well, Immer was a prosperous, prosperous man! His farm was the biggest and best in the entire neighborhood. His fields produced acres of barley and wheat, his vineyards baskets of grapes, his olive trees jars of oil, and his fig trees branches of ripe fruit. *"He thought to himself, 'What should I do, since I don't have anywhere to store my crops?'"* (Luke 12:17). Immer may have inspected his timber and stone barns with an unhappy eye— these buildings were far too small for this year's impressive harvest. This definitely would not do at all. He needed bigger and better, and right away! He probably paced around the buildings measuring the extra space he would need to safely store all his hefty harvest.

"'I will do this,' he said. 'I'll tear down my barns and build bigger ones, and store all my grain and my goods there'" (Luke 12:18). Building new and larger barns would have been a very expensive enterprise, but Immer was very pleased with the idea. He smiled and thought to himself, *"You have many goods stored up for many years. Take it easy; eat, drink, and enjoy yourself"* (Luke 12:19). He sure had his grand plans! From now on his new address could be found on Easy Street.

After all, he had possessions in plenty, and what more could he need or want? (I can think of a few things he needed, but I don't think you'll find them on a shopping list or in a building plan.) Little did Immer realize that he had invited those not-so-welcome guests of greed, envy, dissatisfaction, and pride to move right into his life! Once they move in, they just sort of take over your life and ruin everything that's good and godly. Time to get pest control! (I had the same problem with bookworms last month!)

What did God have to say about all of this preoccupation and self-satisfac-

tion with stuff? *"You fool! This very night your life is demanded of you. And the things you have prepared—whose will they be?"* (Luke 12:20). *Oops!* Immer was clearly rich in stuff, but not so rich in smarts. Jesus warned us, *"One's life is not in the abundance of his possessions"* (Luke 12:15).

What did Immer do wrong? He stored up things for himself but was not rich towards God. Possessions are nice, but they shouldn't be the entire point of our life. That's sort of pointless, don't you think? God had blessed Immer with success and a good life. But was this foolish farmer sharing his blessings with others? No! His plans were all about himself and his own "merry" future—as if he'd done it all himself.

God doesn't want His blessings parked at a dead-end street. His blessings shouldn't stop and get stuck at one person. We are to share our successes! But it's hard to share when greed, envy, dissatisfaction, and pride have been allowed to get way out of control. They don't like to share! They want to keep it all for themselves. Best to get rid of those pests!

God wants us to be rich in the things He treasures, like love, kindness, generosity, and compassion. Those are houseguests you want to have around. Immer could have, and should have, made plans to share some of his success with the community around him. He could have given some of his wealth to help the widow down the block, invested his money to help other farmers, or supported the good things his synagogue did. Giving and sharing should always be part of our present and future plans. Hey, just like I'm sharing these great Bible stories with you!

You can share your success by giving some of the money you earn (from your allowance or odd jobs) to church and to charities so they can help people in need. Don't forget, God gave you that baby-sitting job or that newspaper route! Sharing a little of that earned money is like saying, "Thanks, God!"

Money and things don't have to be the only way you can share your successes. Donating your time and talents is important too. Help

DIDYAKNOW?

Honey made in Jesus' time could still be eaten today. That's an expiration date of thousands of years! WOW!

your school or church organize a charity car wash, bake sale, or bottle drive!

God treasures a caring and giving heart more than all the fortunes in the world! When you work hard and are successful with the things God gives you, God will give you more to care for and share with. Aim to make giving and sharing your main plan.

QUESTION CORNER

- What kind of attitude should you have when you plan for your future?
- Is it important to give? How does the church use your money?
- How can you share what you have with others? Try it out for a week and see how it feels. What happened?

The Important Move

Everybody seems to want to be somebody IMPORTANT these days. Somebody that people want to KNOW, somebody that people want to LOOK at, and somebody people want to be JUST LIKE. People will do almost anything to be on television, interviewed for a magazine, or invited to the really big parties with millionaires, sports heroes, and movie stars. We seem to have gone crazy for fame. This overflow of self-importance isn't a new thing. In fact, it is a very old thing.

Jesus was invited to the house of a very important person in town—a Pharisee, or religious elder and teacher. Everybody who was anybody was at the Pharisee's house. It seems everybody wanted to be the most important person there. They all wanted to sit or stand (or should we say pose?) by their important host. Perhaps they were trying to casually nudge their way to the front of the room. Jesus probably watched this party shuffle for popularity with a knowing smile. What do you think He did? *"He told a parable to those who were invited, when He noticed how they would choose the best places for themselves"* (Luke 14:7).

JOKE

Why are pigs so vain? *They hog all the attention.*

In His story, a wedding feast was taking place, and it seemed like everybody in the village had been invited. Picture this: There was probably entertainment, music, festivities, and tables heaped with good things to eat and drink. People were having a great time; that is, when they weren't trying to nab the seats of honor near the family tables at the front of the room.

Nobody was more eager to sit at the front than a man we'll call Tilon. He had probably spent hours picking out his fine robes for the wedding. Maybe he strutted into the room like a fancy peacock in his colorful flowing robes, wanting everybody to stop and stare, but, most importantly, be pea-green with envy. With eagle-sharp eyes, he must have seen a vacant spot near the wedding table. With a practiced, hurried shuffle, he managed to slide into the chair before another person could claim it. Perhaps he thought, from this spot in the front, everybody would see how wonderful and important he was. Tilon was sooo pleased with himself!

Jesus had this to say, *"When you are invited by someone to a wedding banquet, don't recline at the best place, because a more distinguished person than you may have been invited by your host. The one who invited both of you may come and say to you, 'Give your place to this man,' and then in humiliation, you will proceed to take the lowest place"* (Luke 14:8–9). Oops, how embarrassing!

I guess that's what happened to Tilon. He couldn't believe that the host had actually asked him to sit near the back! Everybody was looking! With a red face, Tilon shuffled to the back and found a seat. He was so ashamed and embarrassed! The wedding host ushered a modest but pleasant looking fellow to the cherished seat in the front. Tilon sank down in his seat; he just wanted to go home.

Here comes the good advice part! Jesus continued His story, *"But when you are invited, go and recline in the lowest place, so that when the one who invited you comes, he will say to you, 'Friend, move up higher.' You will then be honored in the presence of all the other guests. For everyone who exalts himself will be humbled, and the one who humbles himself will be exalted"*

JOKE

Which part of a horse is the most important? *The mane part.*

89

(Luke 14:10–11). How true, how right, how wise!

Why do you think Jesus took that moment to tell that story? Maybe some people in the room needed to learn a lesson in being humble, and maybe they needed to stop thinking about the importance of feeling important! I suppose many of the men at the front squirmed in their seats. They just wanted to go home.

You shouldn't want to be the person who wants to be "important" all the time, and you don't have to put yourself forward. God will put you in situations where your sparkling personality and talent will just naturally shine. So you don't have to worry what other people think about you. God knows how special you are and already has successes planned out for you. Trust God to take care of your spot in life. Humble yourself and God will exalt you.

Say your music teacher has encouraged you to try out for the youth orchestra in your town. Tons of other kids have shown up for the auditions. They all look so confident, and many of them have had more experience! They play sooo well! Suddenly you have that terrible feeling that you're not that good. Maybe you wonder why you even bothered to come out! You just want to go home.

Instead, you find a quiet spot, pray, and ask God to help you get through this knee-shaking experience. You head out on that big stage and put all your faith in God. You lift your flute and play. You feel God's comforting presence all around you. You make only one mistake, and you really feel good about how you did. You are completely surprised and pleased!

Yes! Way to go! You trusted God to help you! That week you get a notice in the mail that the judges were very impressed and you got your spot in the orchestra! Have faith that those special events and successes are all part of God's plan for you. (I was nervous about being your narrator, but I trusted God to help me, and I'm having a great time!) Being important isn't about how people see and value you! It's all about how you respect and value the things God values. That's important! A funny thing happens when you do things God's way: People will respect and admire you. People will be happy and honored to call you "friend." That's the way God made things to work!

QUESTION CORNER

* What is the difference between being confident and being proud? Give some examples.
* How can you humble yourself?
* Did you have an experience where you tried to show off and it didn't work out like you planned? What happened? Would you do things differently next time? How?

Have a Party

"For the Son of Man has come to seek
and to save the lost" (Luke 19:10).

Many people came to listen to Jesus' extraordinary teaching: farmers, fishermen, craftspeople, shopkeepers, women, children, students, soldiers, and (shocked gasp) even tax collectors and sinners. What was wrong with tax collectors? Many people in Israel didn't like them because they got paid well for collecting taxes (for those horrible Romans) and sometimes collected more than they should have and kept it for themselves. I mean, they worked for the Romans! Outraged gasps or not, Jesus didn't care who came to listen. He wanted EVERYBODY to learn about His Father in Heaven.

One day while Jesus was preaching, the Pharisees and teachers of the Law were eyeing the crowd. They didn't like who they saw and began to mutter about Jesus, *"This man welcomes sinners and eats with them"* (Luke 15:2). They might not have liked it, but they were right. Jesus sure did hang out with an interesting mix of friends! Hmmm, can you guess why Jesus taught this lesson that day?

He said, *"What man among you, who has a hundred sheep and loses one of them, does not leave the ninety-nine in the open field and go after the lost one until he finds it?"* (Luke 15:4). Ah, everybody in the crowd understood about shepherds. Why? Many of their great heroes started out as shepherds, like Abraham, Joseph, Moses, and King David. Some of the people in the crowd may have BEEN shepherds themselves.

Can you picture a family of shepherds watering their sheep at a river? As the sheep line up along the banks to drink, the father probably counts them. He counts again. One pregnant ewe is missing. Maybe she wandered off to give birth to her lamb, but alone she could be in serious danger. The father is very concerned. He calls to his son and daughter to watch the flock while he

searches for the lost ewe.

Everybody in the crowd nods their heads in agreement. They would have done the same. Jesus knew they would, *"Does [he] not leave the ninety-nine in the open field and go after the lost one until he finds it?"* (Luke 15:4).

The worried shepherd would have searched all the quiet spots a mother sheep would go. He stops. Did he hear a noise? Searching a dense thicket, he finds the ewe. She is safe and she hasn't given birth yet. Talking softly, he reassures her with his familiar voice and picks her up. He carries her back to the safety of the flock. Soon she will give birth, and he will be there to help her.

JOKE

What do you say when you want a sheep's attention?

"Hey, ewe!"

He is so happy that he jogs home with his heavy bundle.

"When he has found it, he joyfully puts it on his shoulders, and coming home, he calls his friends and neighbors together, saying to them, 'Rejoice with me, because I have found my lost sheep!'" (Luke 15:5–6).

Then Jesus explained the meaning of His seek-and-find illustration. *"I tell you, in the same way, there will be more joy in heaven over one sinner who repents than over ninety-nine righteous people who don't need repentance"* (Luke 15:7). The simple truth is, God loves everyone and actually searches until He finds us. Like the worried shepherd, He wants to keep us safe by His side. God wants everybody to believe in Him and be saved. This was news to the haughty Pharisees. They figured God rejoiced only over them. Why would God fret about sinners and tax collectors? After all, they weren't anybody worth worrying about! Were they? Maybe the Pharisee gang better listen a little more closely.

Clearly, it was very important to Jesus that we understand how much God loves us, because He told a second similar story.

A young bride had carefully put the ten silver coins her fiancée had given her as a wedding present on a chain around her neck. He had worked so hard to get them for her and she loved him very much. Perhaps she was pulling and twisting wool into thread when she suddenly noticed one coin was missing. Oh no! Where could it be? She searched the basket of wool, but it wasn't there. It would have been like losing a diamond out of an engagement ring.

"What woman who has ten silver coins, if she loses one coin, does not light a lamp, sweep the house, and search carefully until she finds it? When she finds it, she calls her women friends and neighbors together, saying, 'Rejoice with me, because I have found the silver coin I lost'" (Luke 15:8–9).

What's the lesson here? To keep a cleaner house? Just kidding! Jesus said, *"I tell you, in the same way, there is joy in the presence of God's angels over one sinner who repents"* (Luke 15:10).

Who was Jesus speaking to when He told these stories? Sure, to the

DIDYAKNOW?

Australia has more sheep than people.

Pharisees to help them get a better perspective. But what about the sinners and tax collectors? He was certainly talking to them too! He wanted to tell everybody—no matter who they were or what they did—that God loves them and will forgive them! God, like a loving father, will desperately seek us out like the shepherd searched for his lost sheep.

We may feel unworthy of God's love, but God doesn't think so. Jesus' message surprised the crowd because it was filled with such love and hope.

You live on a planet with millions and millions of people; why would God worry about little ol' you? Well, He does! God loves YOU! You don't have to be smarter, more popular, or do better at school. You just have to be the special person you already are. You could say you are one in a billion to God. God will look for you, will find you, and really wants a one-on-one relationship with you! God is your heavenly Father! God is so happy when you choose to be with Him. So spend time with God and enjoy that heavenly attention that will last your whole life long. Party on with God! You are No. 1 in His book!

QUESTION CORNER

* How has God sought you out?
* What does it feel like to know that God throws a party in heaven over finding you?
* What kind of party would you want?

That's My Boy

Do you know why life isn't like a video or computer game? In a game, when we make the wrong choices and wind up facing the galactic sludge-monster, we can always go back and fix things. Push a button and restart the game. We can't restart life, so we have to make careful choices. Here's a parable on growing up and making those choices. Let's take a closer look at the people in the story.

"'A man had two sons" (Luke

15:11). As brothers go (let's call them Ira and Joel), these two were worlds apart! Ira was a hardworking guy who was content to spend his life on the farm. Younger brother, Joel, couldn't wait to get off the farm and explore the world. Farming was boring! Adventure was calling, and he was ready to get out there and party hearty.

"The younger of them said to his father, 'Father, give me the share of the estate I have coming to me.' So he distributed the assets to them. Not many days later, the younger son gathered together all he had and traveled to a distant country, where he squandered his estate in foolish living" (Luke 15:12–13). He had a good time while it lasted. I imagine the first thing he did

was buy a fast horse! Joel soon became the life of each and every party in every town he raced into. Well, the horse probably didn't last long, because Joel gambled it away in a dice game. And neither did his money. Joel was sure things would turn around in his favor. But life in the fast lane was heading for a big crash.

"After he had spent everything, a severe famine struck that country, and he had nothing" (Luke 15:14).

Joel sure made some bad choices and was left with a big nothing. But this is life, and he couldn't push restart. What did he do? *"He went to work for one of the citizens of that country, who sent him into his fields to feed pigs"* (Luke 15:15). Not exactly the glamour and adventure he was looking for. Now that his money had run out, his only friends were swine. Really! They were actual oink-grunting,

tail-curling, mud-slinging pigs. He was knee-deep in a muddy situation and sinking fast! *"He longed to eat his fill from the carob pods the pigs were eating, and no one would give him any"* (Luke 15:16). Eating pig food and sleeping in mud! If this *were* a computer game, I'd quit. Which is actually pretty close to what he did do.

"When he came to his senses, he said, 'How many of my father's hired hands have more than enough food, and here I am dying of hunger! I'll get up, go to my father, and say to him, "Father, I have sinned against heaven and in your sight.

I'm no longer worthy to be called your son. Make me like one of your hired hands."' So he got up and went to his father" (Luke 15:17–20). That was probably the smartest move this guy had made in a long time.

Meanwhile, back at the farm, things were going well, but dear old Dad sure missed his younger boy. Joel was a handful sometimes, but he was a good boy at heart. *"While the son was still a long way off, his father saw him and was filled with compassion. He ran, threw his arms around his neck, and kissed him. The son said to him, 'Father, I have sinned against heaven and your sight. I'm no longer worthy to be called your son.'*

"But the father told his slaves, 'Quick! Bring out the best robe and put it on him; put a ring on his finger and sandals on his feet. Then bring the fatted calf and slaughter it, and let's celebrate with a feast,

because this son of mine was dead and is alive again; he was lost and is found.' So they began to celebrate" (Luke 20–24). The father may have been disappointed in Joel, but that didn't take away from the love he felt for him. God's the same way! He loves us no matter what!

But all was not happy on the old homestead. *"Now his older son was in the field; as he came near the house, he heard music and dancing. So he summoned one of the servants and asked what these things meant. 'Your brother is here,' he told him, 'and your father has slaughtered the fatted calf because he has him back safe and sound'"* (Luke 15:25–27). Ira could hardly believe his ears! He worked hard every single day of every single year without complaint or demands, and his father barely seemed to notice! This wasn't fair! This really stunk! And it wasn't just the fact that his brother smelled like a pig!

Well, big brother wasn't exactly ready to say, "Howdy, little bro." *"He became angry and didn't want to go in. So his father came out and pleaded with him.*

"But he replied to his father, 'Look, I have been slaving many years for you, and I have never disobeyed your orders; yet you never gave me a young goat so I could celebrate with my friends. But when this son of yours came, who has devoured your assets . . . you slaughtered the fatted calf for him'" (Luke 15:28–30). Ira was feeling a tad undervalued. He just didn't understand how much his father loved them both!

"'Son,' he said to him, 'you are always with me, and everything I have is yours. But

JOKE

Why was the computer so tired when it got home? *Because it had a hard drive!*

we had to celebrate and rejoice, because this brother of yours was dead and is alive again; he was lost and is found'" (Luke 15:31–32).

The younger son didn't do a whole lot of planning. He ran on big time impulsiveness and did wrong things. It seems he wanted a full-time dose of fun and thrills. Hey, a roller-coaster is fun for the first five rides, but soon your stomach's doing flip-flops, and you want to get off big time. That's the same with Joel! He wanted full-time adventure, but that's not what he ended up with, was it?

God wants you to do right things all the time and make smart, godly choices. When you're playing a computer or video game, who makes the game choices? You do, of course. Life is the same. God lets you choose how you want to live your life. He doesn't butt in and play the game for you. He waits for you to seek His advice when you come to those moments of choice. You get His advice by following the directions He has given you in the Bible. You can also pray and seek wise counsel from godly people you know. All these things help you find God's direction for your life. God's talking to you. You just have to stop and learn how to listen. When you do follow His way, it always works out the best. God's a high scorer when it comes to the game of life.

QUESTION CORNER

* If you follow God's direction, does that mean nothing bad can happen to you?
* Have you ever chosen to do your own thing instead of what was right? What happened?
* How does it feel to know God loves you even when you make mistakes?

Manage to Be Godly

"So if you have not been faithful with the unrighteous money, who will trust you with what is genuine?" (Luke 16:11).

Have you got savvy? You know, smarts or resourcefulness? That's okay if you don't know. Sometimes we don't find out whether we have them until we need them. Jesus understood that we live in a world that doesn't understand a whole lot about heaven, but works overtime looking for success and money. This parable tells you all about it.

"There was a rich man who received an accusation that his manager was squan-

dering his possessions. So he called the manager in and asked, 'What is this I hear about you? Give an account of your management, because you can no longer be my manager'" (Luke 16:1–2). Let's call this tricky manager Ezer. Ezer may have tried looking surprised, then confused, maybe even shocked, but in the end he only looked guilty. It was true Ezer had done some less-than-honest accounting for his master. Perhaps he had told his master that he sold their wine for ten denarii, when actually he had received twelve. He had pocketed the extra two. Now his hand was firmly caught in the cookie jar, and you could say his life was

TRIVIA

Israelites gave back to God how much of their income? *Ten percent.*

crumbling around him. He suddenly found himself discharged, dismissed, let go, sent packing, dropped, and fired. I think we should throw the book at him. (But not my book!)

But crafty Ezer was always looking for the easy way out. He cast his shifty eyes on the people who owed his master money. Ezer was about to play a very sleazy game of "Let's Make A Dishonest Deal." *"The manager said to himself, 'What should I do, since my master is taking the management away from me? I'm not strong enough to dig; I'm ashamed to beg. I know what I'll do so that when I'm removed from management, people will welcome me into their homes"* (Luke 16:3–4).

What he did next was again on the very shady side of not-so-honest.

"He summoned each one of his master's debtors. 'How much do you owe my master?' he asked the first one. 'A hundred measures of oil,' he said.

"'Take your invoice,' he told him, 'sit down quickly, and write fifty'" (Luke 16:5–6). Wait a minute! Turn on that calculator again! That little rascal Ezer did the same for each one of his master's debtors. He cut their debts so that they would like him and would take him into their home when he got the big boot out of his master's house. Ezer was worldly, but was he right? Big "NO" on that one. Yet we're told to be like him. Not exactly like him. Let me explain.

You see, many people in this world aren't really interested in, or don't even respect, what God thinks is right. They respect the person who is a sly businessman, a shrewd tycoon, and who can look out for No. 1. Jesus wanted us to understand the nature of the world we live in. You know the old saying, "It's a jungle out there." We should always do things the way God wants us to, but we should also be aware that not everybody is going to try to be as good, ethical, honest, and compassionate as we have been taught to be.

Jesus doesn't want us to be worldly smart—He wants us to be godly smart. Ezer knew how to make worldly friends. God wants us to learn how to make eternal friends. How? Just do things the way God would. Help people out. Be kind and generous. You know, kind of like what Ezer tried to do sneakily, but do it from a heart of love. We can be wiser than Ezer. He knew he'd need friends. We need friends too, but let's make sure we have the right kind; *God's* kind. When we help people out and love them, they'll listen to us. We can share with them about our relationship with God. Then they can have a never-ending relationship with Him too. Talk about eternal friends!

"Whoever is faithful in very little is also faithful in much; and whoever is unrighteous in very little is also unrighteous in much" (Luke 16:10).

It is important to be honest with everybody and in everything you do. If Ezer had actually done a good job in the first place, he wouldn't need to buy friendships. Good friends come free of charge! God wants to bless you with good friends, a loving home, and a happy life. Remember, doing it God's way means making right choices. If you can't be trusted in little everyday things, how can God trust you with the really important things He wants you to do in life?

"If you have not been faithful with the unrighteous money, who will trust you with what is genuine? And if you have not been faithful with what belongs to someone else, who will give you what is your own?" (Luke 16:11–12).

You can't be a little honest. You either ARE honest, or you are NOT

JOKE

Why did the olive tree go to the dentist? *To get a root canal.*

honest. Honesty doesn't just happen. Honesty is a homegrown asset! Suppose a friend was doing badly in school and offered you money to do his homework or take a test for him—nobody should find out. He'd get a better grade, and you'd get a little money. Who's it really going to hurt?

Sneaky Ezer found out that all his troubles started the moment he figured dishonesty pays. And now he's facing payback time. He's heading into big-time hurt!

Dishonesty hurts YOU! Jesus says, *"No servant can be the slave of two masters, since either he will hate one and love the other, or he will be devoted to one and despise the other. You can't be slaves to both God and money"* (Luke16:13).

You have to choose between doing right and doing wrong. Doing things God's way is a-hundred-and-one-percent-for-certain-absolutely-giving-it-your-all kind of thing. No more sitting on the fence, waffling, or "maybe I'll be godly tomorrow." Be certain, choose wisely, be generous, and do the things that honor God.

QUESTION CORNER

❊ How can you make eternal friends?
❊ What is our reward for living a right life?
❊ What types of things are you trusted with? How do you handle them?

Knock, Knock

"So I say to you, keep asking, and it will be given to you. Keep searching, and you will find. Keep knocking, and the door will be opened to you. For everyone who asks receives, and the one who searches finds, and to the one who knocks, the door will be opened" (Luke 11:9–10).

'm going to tell you what persistence is. No, really, I'm going to tell you about persistence. Look, LET ME just tell you what persistence means! There, you see, that's persistence! It means doing something in spite of great obstacles.

Here's why persistence is a good thing! (I'm going to fill out the story a bit.)

"Suppose one of you has a friend and goes to him at midnight and says to him, 'Friend, lend me three loaves of bread, because a friend of mine on a journey has

come to me, and I don't have anything to offer him'" (Luke 11:5–6).

Sadly there were no 24-hour corner stores or Seven-Elevens in Jesus' time. So here's this poor guy (we'll call him Issie) hosting a horde of hungry travelers with one musty piece of bread and a thimble of sour goat's milk. Yuck! What to do? What to do? Ah! Issie remembered his baker friend (call him Neth). Neth had tons of bread at his house! Issie decided to rush over there and pay a call on his good ol' pal. Besides, Neth wouldn't mind a friendly visit in the middle of

the night. What are friends for?

Neth probably tried to ignore the pounding on his door! He pulled his blankets up over his ears, but the pounding only got louder. What inconsiderate, camel-headed lout would be waking people up at this hour? Then he heard Issie's voice calling through the window! Oh, that explains it! Poor Neth couldn't believe this late-night mooching. Can't a man get a good night's sleep around here? *"Then he will answer from inside and say, 'Don't bother me! The door is already locked, and my children and I have gone to bed. I can't get up to give you anything'"* (Luke 11:7). Well, Issie kept knocking until a sleepy-eyed Neth opened the door and gave it to him. I mean, he really threw the bread at him! Good thing Issie ducked!

Jesus' story goes on to tell us that Issie got his bread, not because of his friendship with his sleepy friend, but because he was bold enough to go knocking at the door at midnight. His late-night borrowing earned him as much as he wanted.

This story doesn't give you the license to go pounding on everyone's door at all hours, but there is a special friend's door that is open any time you want to knock. God is there for you day or night. Bring to God your needs, thanks, concerns, problems, and love. His door is always open.

"He then told them a parable on the need for them to pray always and not become discouraged: 'There was a judge in one town who didn't fear God or respect man. And a widow in that town kept coming to him, saying, "Give me justice against my adversary"'" (Luke 18:1–3). Let's take a look at the people in this story. There was a highly regarded judge—let's name him Sol. He understood the Law and daily made important decisions regarding people's lives. When Sol walked down the street, people got out of his way. Here comes the judge! He was the man in charge, and he made sure everybody knew it. He was a one-man, self-important legal team.

There was in this town a widow—let's call her Abby. Abby worked hard to keep her little family together. But I guess many people tried to take advantage of her husbandless situation.

JOKE

What is the fastest mountain in the world?
Mt. Rushmore.

Perhaps a neighboring farmer was trying to force her to sell her prize oxen. He made threats and made her life difficult every day. But Abby was no pushover. She wasn't about to be bulldozed, or should we say plowed over, into giving up the only thing of value she had left. Every day, Abby stood in front of Judge Sol's house because she wanted her bullying neighbor to stop bothering her! Judge Sol was getting fairly tired of seeing her determined face every morning and every night. It was giving him nightmares! A man can only take so much. Something had to give!

"For a while he was unwilling; but later he said to himself, 'Even though I don't fear God or respect man, yet because this widow keeps pestering me, I will give her justice, so she doesn't wear me out by her persistent coming'" (Luke 18:4–5).

Abby, because of her persistence, won herself justice. Her oxen-eyeing neighbor was told to stop. A court order! Abby got justice, not because Judge Sol was particularly honest or caring, but because he was completely PESTERED. He just wanted to get rid of her!

God is sooo different from that self-important judge! He really cares about our problems and concerns. He wants to help us, not because we bother Him, but because He loves us. We never have to picket or hold a big rally at God's house to get His attention! When we truly need Him, God will get into the action and help us.

JOKE

What is the slowest mountain in the world?

Mt. Ever-rest.

"Will not God grant justice to His elect who cry out to Him day and night? Will He delay to help them? I tell you that He will swiftly grant them justice. Nevertheless, when the Son of Man comes, will He find that faith on earth?" (Luke 18:7–8).

Your job is to trust God with your problems and to not be afraid to discuss them with Him whenever and wherever you need to. God wants to keep those lines of communication open! Prayer is your phone line to God, and you never get a busy signal, get put on hold, or have to leave a message. God doesn't mind if you talk to Him about the same old problems or needs. He enjoys long heart-to-hearts with you. Pray on the school bus, while skiing, or when you have problems, day or night. God is there instantly in every situation. God's waiting for your prayer call, so don't put Him on hold!

QUESTION CORNER

- Are there some needs or situations that you have been nervous about talking to God about? Be bold and talk to Him about them now!
- Why are you tempted to stop praying? Why should you continue to pray?
- Why will God answer your prayers?

I'm Not Practically Perfect in Every Way?

"He leads the humble in the right path, and He teaches the humble His way. All the paths of the Lord are grace and truth to those who keep His covenant and His commands" (Psalm 25:9–10).

How would you like to hang out with a friend that said this all day? "I'm so wonderful, I'm so smart, I'm so special, I'm good at everything, I'm pretty and talented, and clever, and honest, and, and, and . . ."

Pretty boring right?

"He told this parable to some who trusted in themselves that they were righteous and looked down on everyone else: 'Two men went up to the temple complex to pray, one a Pharisee and the other a tax collector'"

117

(Luke 18:9–10). Remember, a Pharisee was a religious leader and teacher. We could call this important guy Jakim. The tax collector was a guy who, well, collected taxes (money) for the Roman government and sometimes collected more for himself. Nobody really respected or liked him. Let's call this I-can't-get-no-respect guy Danny. On with the story.

Here's how I think it went down. Jakim strode into the temple like a man who owned the place. This was his stage, and he was a star! He liked it that the other worshippers thought he was an important religious guy. After all, he prayed a lot, thought deep religious thoughts, and looked pretty good in his designer robes. *"The Pharisee took his stand and was praying like this: 'God, I thank You that I'm not like other people—greedy, unrighteous, adulterers, or even like this tax collector. I fast twice a week; I give a tenth of everything I get'"* (Luke 18:11–12). Okay, humble wasn't exactly Jakim's middle name.

Enter stage . . . I mean temple gate right. I picture Danny the tax collector peeking around the corner to make sure nobody would notice him enter the temple. Maybe he inched through the door and found a quiet spot by himself. He didn't want to hear the nasty names the other worshippers hissed at him as he walked by. It probably made Danny so nervous to go there. But this

JOKE

Why did the scientist install a knocker on his door? *To win the Nobel (no bell) prize!*

was God's temple and Danny needed God. It didn't help that the great Pharisee Jakim always stared and frowned at him. I figure Danny knew what he was and wasn't proud of it, but he wanted and needed to pray to God. *"The tax collector, standing far off, would not even raise his eyes to heaven, but kept striking his chest and saying, 'O God, turn your wrath from me—a sinner!'"* (Luke 18:13).

Which man do you think honored and pleased God with his attitude? What? No votes for our well-dressed Pharisee? Okay, you're right; he isn't exactly a role model! Jesus had this to say about the modest tax collector, *"I tell you, this one went down to his house justified rather than the other; because everyone who exalts himself will be humbled, but the one who humbles himself will be exalted"* (Luke 18:14).

God forgave humble Danny because he truly WAS sorry for the mistakes he had made. Did the Pharisee even think he had committed any mistakes? Nope, he felt he was practically perfect in every way. Well, I'll let you in on a little secret—that attitude is a huge mistake. Only God is truly perfect. The moment we start thinking how saintly we are and how perfect we are is exactly the same moment we disappoint God. How can God help someone who doesn't want or think they need help? The Pharisee was very impressed with himself. He was a

> **TRIVIA**
>
> What did Jesus want the temple of God to be called? *A house of prayer* (Matthew 21:15).

120

superstar in his own mind! Jakim really had no place on his stage . . . I mean life . . . for God.

Talk to many doctors, athletes, scientists, and other dedicated and successful people, and many will tell you they don't actually know how they do the amazing things they do. Many will say that they believe God was there helping them achieve their goals and directing their lives. The important thing is to recognize that you need God in your life. Everything good in your life comes from God! Give God the credit!

God doesn't look at outward things! God looks at what's in your heart. Often magazines will select individuals to be on a Top Ten list of successful people. Many of them are glamorous, rich, and popular. But would they be on God's list of successful people? Maybe not! *"The Lord doesn't see as people see. For people look at the outer appearance, but the Lord looks at the heart"* (1 Samuel 16:7). Maybe a person on God's list would be the little old lady in New York who sits in her apartment and knits baby bootees for orphans in other countries. Maybe it would be that pig farmer who sets aside money so needy children can go to summer Bible camp. He hasn't had a vacation of his own in years! Working with pigs doesn't bring glamour and fame, but his heart is sooo clean and beautiful to God. God's superstars are just ordinary people with extraordinary spirits, who have set their faith and love in

DIDYAKNOW?

Over 1,784 million people in the world follow Jesus' teachings.

God's hands. How do you get on God's Top Ten list? First off, have a humble heart and rely on God. He'll teach you and tell you how to be a person who is successful where it counts. When you do things God's way, you are always a winner. Don't forget to make room in your life for God.

QUESTION CORNER

- Why do some people seem more successful than others? Is it because they pray harder? Are they really more successful?
- What is God's measure of success?
- Who do you want to be like, Jakim or Danny? Why? How can you do that?

The Net

"Again, the kingdom of heaven is like a large net thrown into the sea. It collected every kind of fish, and when it was full, they dragged it ashore, sat down, and gathered the good fish into containers, but threw out the worthless ones. So it will be at the end of the age" (Matthew 13:47–49).

Hey why don't you go check out the net! No, not the Internet! Jesus often used fishing as a way of explaining heavenly matters.

It's time to ask ourselves, in the big lake of life, "What kind of fish am I?" Am I the kind of person Jesus wants to keep, or am I the kind who isn't very useful and gets thrown away?

How do you become a keeper? Learn the way God wants you to live your life and then do it! If you need more details, read the Bible and ask a ton of questions! Pretty soon you'll have an entire net full of godly knowledge that you can share. Hey, you are the catch of the day!

QUESTION CORNER

- Think of twenty questions about God you always wanted to know. List them and see how many answers you can find.

No Applause Please!

"Which one of you having a slave plowing or tending sheep, would say to him when he comes in from the field, 'Come at once and sit down to eat'? Instead, would he not tell him, 'Prepare something for me to eat, get ready, and serve me while I eat and drink; later you may eat and drink'? Does he thank that slave because he did what he was commanded?" (Luke 17:7–9).

If praise is your main reason for helping others or doing right things, then you had better rethink why you do things. Praise shouldn't be your goal. Jesus viewed His amazing life as just doing His duty.

Don't expect a cheerleading squad to jump through hoops every time you do normal chores, or for a flashing, neon arrow to point to you every time you do something good.

Instead, do good things because that's what God wants you to do. Doing God's will is just part of your daily routine. Remember, it's just all in a day's work.

QUESTION CORNER:

☀ What types of things are just part of your godly duties?

Fair Enough!

If you think that verse is a little confusing now, it won't be by the end of this parable.

"For the kingdom of heaven is like a landowner who went out early in the morning to hire workers for his vineyard. After agreeing with the workers on one denarius for the day" (Matthew 20:1–2), the landowner went out to the marketplace and found more workers. At the end of the day, each worker was given his promised denarius. But the ones who'd worked all day thought they deserved more!

The landowner explained. *"Didn't you agree with me on a denarius? Take what's yours and go. . . . Don't I have the right to do what I want with my business?"* (Matthew 20:13–15).

God is just as generous as that landowner. We don't have to compete for His attention, because God loves us equally. What matters is that we contribute our best efforts. God wants us to willingly serve Him, do our best, and learn more about Him. So, who cares if they are first or last! There are no line-ups for God's love.

QUESTION CORNER:

* How would you have felt if you had been the first workers? The last? Why?

Thanks For Inviting Me!

"But as it is written: What no eye has seen and no ear has heard, and what has never come into a man's heart, is what God has prepared for those who love Him" (1 Corinthians 2:9).

What if you threw a party and nobody came? A man prepared a party and invited many people. They said they could come but then made last minute excuses. The man told his servant, *"Go out quickly into the streets and alleys of the city, and bring in here the poor, maimed, blind, and lame!"* (Luke 14:21). Soon the house was full of grateful people.

Did you know? Everybody is invited to the biggest party ever! How do we get to that party? Accept Jesus and love God with all our hearts! Simple!

But still, some people make excuses. They don't think they need God or maybe He doesn't fit into their lifestyles. God will fill His house with grateful people, not excuses. Those who refuse His invitation now will not be allowed into His kingdom later.

God wants you to RSVP ASAP. Stop and say, "Thanks! I'd love to come!"

QUESTION CORNER:

* How does accepting God's invitation change your life?

Conclusion

Hard to believe, but we've come to the end of our journey. I've really had a good time exploring the parables with you. Through Jesus' stories I hope you've learned a lot about the people back then, and about the challenges they faced.

You also have a heap of treasure to take home with you. What? You didn't notice us collecting it as we went along? Well, that's okay. This type of treasure won't make you wealthy. You've learned what God values. That's exactly the gift Jesus wanted to leave with you! Don't forget, if you lose it, you know exactly where to find it again. This treasure never runs out. In fact, you can give it away to others and have even more.

So, get out into the world and share Jesus' stories with a friend. Then they can have treasure too! Thanks for dropping by, and thanks for laughing at my jokes! Until next time, God bless, and see you around.

LIGHTwave
building Christian faith in families

Lightwave Publishing is one of North America's leading developers of quality resources that encourage, assist, and equip parents to build Christian faith in their families. Their products help parents answer their children's questions about the Christian faith, teach them how to make church, Sunday school, and Bible reading more meaningful for their children, provide them with pointers on teaching their children to pray, and much, much more.

Lightwave, together with its various publishing and ministry partners, such as Focus on the Family, has been successfully producing innovative books, music, and games for the past 15 years. Some of their more recent products include *A Parents' Guide to the Spiritual Growth of Children*, *Joy Ride!*, *Mealtime Moments*, and *My Time With God*.

Lightwave also has a fun kids' Web site and an Internet-based newsletter called *Tips and Tools for Spiritual Parenting*. For more information and a complete list of Lightwave products, please visit: **www.lightwavepublishing.com**.